The Knock Out
Knock Knock
Joke Book

By Gyles Brandreth

Illustrations by John MacGregor

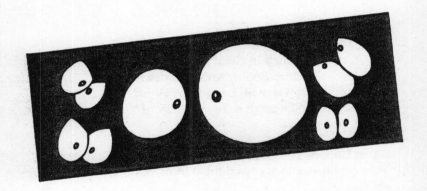

MADCAP

Published in Great Britain in 1998 by
Madcap Books, André Deutsch Ltd,
76 Dean St, London, W1V 5HA
André Deutsch is a subsidiary of VCI plc

A catalogue record for this title is available
from the British Library

ISBN 0 233 99376 2

Knock, knock.
Who's there?
Dewey.
Dewey who?
Dewey have to listen to all these knock-
knock jokes?

Knock, knock.
Who's there?
X.
X who?
X-tremely pleased to meet you.

Knock, knock.
Who's there?
Warren.
Warren who?
Warren Peace is a famous Russian novel.

Knock, knock.
Who's there?
Tank.
Tank who?
My pleasure.

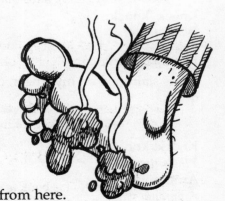

Knock, knock.
Who's there?
Sonya.
Sonya who?
Sonya foot, I smell it from here.

Knock, knock.
Who's there?
Ivory.
Ivory who?
Ivory strong, how strong are you?

Knock, knock.
Who's there?
Philippa.
Philippa who?
Philippa bathtub, I'm dirty.

Knock, knock.
Who's there?
Oscar.
Oscar who?
Oscar stupid question, you get a stupid
answer.

Knock, knock.
Who's there?
Doris.
Doris who?
Doris slammed on my finger, open up
quick.

Knock, knock.
Who's there?
Ammonia.
Ammonia who?
Ammonia little boy who can't reach the
doorbell.

Knock, knock.
Who's there?
Norma Lee.
Norma Lee who?
Norma Lee I wouldn't have troubled you,
but I need help.

Knock, knock.
Who's there?
An author.
An author who?
An author joke like this and I'm off!

Knock, knock.
Who's there?
Plato.
Plato who?
Plato fish and chips
please.

Knock, knock.
Who's there?
Butter.
Butter who?
Butter be quick, I have to go to the
bathroom.

Knock, knock.
Who's there?
Seth.
Seth who?
Seth me, and what I seth goes.

Knock, knock.
Who's there?
Alec.
Alec who?
Alec coffee, but I don't like tea.

Knock, knock.
Who's there?
Ellie.
Ellie who?
Ellie phants never forget.

Knock, knock.
Who's there?
Disc.
Disc who?
Disc is a recorded message...

Knock, knock.
Who's there?
Victor.
Victor who?
Victor his trousers
climbing over
the fence.

Knock, knock.
Who's there?
Michelle.
Michelle who?
Michelle had a big
crab inside it.

Knock, knock.
Who's there?
Francis.
Francis who?
Francis the other
side of the Channel.

Knock, knock.
Who's there?
Cook.
Cook who?
That's the first I've heard this year.

Knock, knock.
Who's there?
Thermos.
Thermos who?
Thermos be a better knock-knock joke
than this.

Knock, knock.
Who's there?
Juicy.
Juicy who?
Juicy what I just saw?

7

Knock, knock.
Who's there?
Pizza.
Pizza who?
Pizza cake would be great right now.

Knock, knock.
Who's there?
Fletcher
Fletcher who?
Fletcher self go.

Knock, knock.
Who's there?
Fitzwilliam.
Fitzwilliam who?
Fitzwilliam better than it fits me.

Knock, knock.
Who's there?
Paul Aidy.
Paul Aidy who?
Paul Aidy, she
trippedand fell
in the mud.

Knock, knock.
Who's there?
Celeste.
Celeste who?
Celeste time I do your homework.

Knock, knock.
Who's there?
Dozen.
Dozen who?
Dozen anyone live here
any more?

Knock, knock.
Who's there?
Butcher.
Butcher who?
Butcher left leg in, your left leg out...

Knock, knock.
Who's there?
Sherwood.
Sherwood who?
Sherwood like to help you out, which way
did you come in?

Knock, knock.
Who's there?
Jennie.
Jennie who?
Jennie-d any help
opening the door?

Knock, knock.
Who's there?
Fred.
Fred who?
Fred I'm going to have to leave now.

Knock, knock.
Who's there?
Sicily.
Sicily who?
Sicily question to ask.

Knock, knock.
Who's there?
Europe.
Europe who?
Europe to no good.

Knock, knock.
Who's there?
Spider.
Spider who?
Spider when she
thought I wasn't
looking.

Knock, knock.
Who's there?
Hal.
Hal who?
Hallo to you too!

Knock, knock.
Who's there?
Anne.
Anne who?
Anne Tartic is at the South
Pole.

Knock, knock.
Who's there?
Yelp.
Yelp who?
Yelp me! My nose is stuck in the keyhole!

Knock, knock.
Who's there?
Sizzle.
Sizzle who?
Sizzle hurt me more than it will you.

Knock, knock.
Who's there?
Midas.
Midas who?
Midas well open the door 'cos I'm not
going away.

Knock, knock.
Who's there?
Conan.
Conan who?
Conan wafers go
well with ice-cream.

Knock, knock.
Who's there?
Farmer.
Farmer who?
Farmer birthday I'm going to have a new
bike.

Knock, knock.
Who's there?
Buddha.
Buddha who?
Buddha this slice of bread for me, please.

Knock, knock.
Who's there?
Dewitt.
Dewitt who?
Dewitt now or never.

Knock, knock.
Who's there?
Gutter.
Gutter who?
Gutter get in, it's
snowing out here.

Knock, knock.
Who's there?
Pot.
Pot who?
Pot T. about you.

Knock, knock.
Who's there?
Cash.
Cash who?
They're my favourite nuts!

Knock, knock.
Who's there?
Murray.
Murray who?
Murray me! Not likely!

Knock, knock.
Who's there?
Dinosaur.
Dinosaur who?
Dinosaur with you
because you called her stupid.

Knock, knock.
Who's there?
Element.
Element who?
Element to tell you she can't see you
today.

Knock, knock.
Who's there?
Dog.
Dog who?
Doggone it, open the door!

Knock, knock.
Who's there?
Lydia.
Lydia who?
Lydia dustbin
just blew away.

Knock, knock.
Who's there?
Rabbit.
Rabbit who?
Rabbit up nicely, it's a present.

Knock, knock.
Who's there?
Bless.
Bless who?
I didn't sneeze!

Knock, knock.
Who's there?
Edith.
Edith who?
Edith'd me on the lipth.

Knock, knock.
Who's there?
Aldous.
Aldous who?
Aldous who want to leave the room, put
your hand up.

Knock, knock.
Who's there?
Amelia.
Amelia who?
With my cooking
it's Amelia never
going to forget.

Knock, knock.
Who's there?
Doris.
Doris who?
Doris dropping off its
hinges with all this
knocking.

Knock, knock.
Who's there?
Diesel.
Diesel who?
Diesel teach you to go around knocking
on doors.

Knock, knock.
Who's there?
Percy.
Percy who?
Percy Vere and you'll succeed.

Knock, knock.
Who's there?
Adeline.
Adeline who?
Adeline extra to the letter.

Knock, knock.
Who's there?
Teacher.
Teacher who?
Teacher to go knocking
on my door in the
middle of the night.

Knock, knock.
Who's there?
Nose.
Nose who?
I nose plenty more knock-knock jokes,
don't worry!

Knock, knock.
Who's there?
Eggs.
Eggs who?
Eggstremely cold waiting for you to open
the door.

Knock, knock.
Who's there?
Barry.
Barry who?
Barry your bone in the garden, little dog.

Knock, knock.
Who's there?
Harold
Harold who?
Hark the Harold Angels sing.

Knock, knock.
Who's there?
Philip.
Philip who?
Philip the tank, I've
got a long way to go.

Knock, knock.
Who's there?
Canoe.
Canoe who?
Canoe come out and play?

Knock, knock.
Who's there?
Money.
Money who?
Money is stiff since I
knockedit on the table leg.

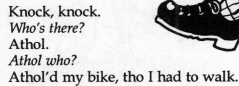

Knock, knock.
Who's there?
Athol.
Athol who?
Athol'd my bike, tho I had to walk.

Knock, knock.
Who's there?
Lloyd.
Lloyd who?
He Lloyd to me, he said it was
Wednesday and it's only Tuesday!

Knock, knock.
Who's there?
Derek.
Derek who?
'Derek of the Hesperus' is a famous poem
by Longfellow.

Knock, knock.
Who's there?
Harriet.
Harriet who?
Harriet all my lunch,
I'm starving.

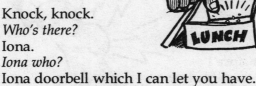

Knock, knock.
Who's there?
Iona.
Iona who?
Iona doorbell which I can let you have.

Knock, knock.
Who's there?
Europe.
Europe who?
Europe early
this morning.

Knock, knock.
Who's there?
Juno.
Juno who?
Of course I do!Knock, knock.

Who's there?
Old King Cole.
Old King Cole who?
Old King Cole, so turn the heat up.

Knock, knock.
Who's there?
Yolande.
Yolande who?
Yolande me a pound, I'll pay you back
next week.

Knock, knock.
Who's there?
Colin.
Colin who?
Colin and see me on your way home.

Knock, knock.
Who's there?
Diana.
Diana who?
Diana thirst, can
I have some water
please?

Knock, knock.
Who's there?
Olga.
Olga who?
Olga home if you don't open up.

Knock, knock.
Who's there?
Watson.
Watson who?
Watson your mind?

Knock, knock.
Who's there?
Flo.
Flo who?
Flo Ting down
the river.

Knock, knock.
Who's there?
Earl.
Earl who?
Earl be glad to tell you if you open the
door.

Knock, knock.
Who's there?
Roxanne.
Roxanne who?
Roxanne pebbles are all over this beach.

Knock, knock.
Who's there?
Alex.
Alex who?
Alex Plain later.

Knock, knock.
Who's there?
Euripedes.
Euripedes who?
Euripedes pants and you'll pay for a new pair!

Knock, knock.
Who's there?
Eumenides.
Eumenides who?
Eumenides trousers and I won't tell that
you ripped them.

Knock, knock.
Who's there?
Isadore.
Isadore who?
Isadore open or locked?

Knock, knock.
Who's there?
Tuba.
Tuba who?
Tuba toothpaste.

Knock, knock.
Who's there?
Wafer.
Wafer who?
Wafer a long time, but here I am again.

Knock, knock.
Who's there?
Ewan.
Ewan who?
No one, just me.

Knock, knock.
Who's there?
Abyssinia.
Abyssinia who?
Abyssinia when I get back.

Knock, knock.
Who's there?
Sacha.
Sacha who?
Sacha lot of fuss about nothing.

Knock, knock.
Who's there?
Mischa.
Mischa who?
Mischa a lot.

Knock, knock.
Who's there?
Stella.
Stella who?
Stella no answer at the door.

Knock, knock.
Who's there?
Twain.
Twain who?
Twains are what wabbits take twips on.

Knock, knock.
Who's there?
Robin.
Robin who?
Robin the piggy
bank again.

Knock, knock.
Who's there?
Candy.
Candy who?
Candy cow jumps over the moon?

Knock, knock.
Who's there?
Button.
Button who?
Button in is not polite.

Knock, knock.
Who's there?
Yah.
Yah who?
Ride 'em cowboy!

Knock, knock.
Who's there?
Buster.
Buster who?
Buster school, please.

Knock, knock.
Who's there?
Ida.
Ida who?
Ida know. Sorry!

Knock, knock.
Who's there?
Fanny.
Fanny who?
Fanny body calls, I'm out.

Knock, knock.
Who's there?
Don.
Don who?
Don just stand there, say something.

Knock, knock.
Who's there?
Rhoda.
Rhoda who?
Rhoda boat as fast as you can.

Knock, knock.
Who's there?
Aldous
Aldous who?
Aldous who aren't interested – go home.

Knock, knock.
Who's there?
Voodoo.
Voodoo who?
Voodoo you think
you are, Superman?

Knock, knock.
Who's there?
Oscar.
Oscar who?
Oscar if she wants a drink.

Knock, knock.
Who's there?
Turnip.
Turnip who?
Turnip the heat,
it's cold in here.

Knock, knock.
Who's there?
Manny.
Manny who?
Manny are called, but few are chosen.

Knock, knock.
Who's there?
Brigham.
Brigham who?
Brigham back as soon as you can.

Knock, knock.
Who's there?
Wound.
Wound who?
Wound and wound the wugged wocks the
wagged wascal wan.

Knock, knock.
Who's there?
Bigotry.
Bigotry who?
Bigotry than the one in your garden.

Knock, knock.
Who's there?
Pill.
Pill who?
Yes, please, and a
sheet to go with it.

Knock, knock.
Who's there?
Love.
Love who?
Love you too, Honeybunch.

Knock, knock.
Who's there?
Holmes.
Holmes who?
Holmes sweet home.

Knock, knock.
Who's there?
Tads.
Tads who?
Tads all, folks!

Knock, knock.
Who's there?
Havana.
Havana who?
Havana wonderful time,
wish you werehere.

Knock, knock.
Who's there?
Zombies.
Zombies who?
Zombies make honey,
others are drones.

Knock, knock.
Who's there?
Gladys.
Gladys who?
Gladys Friday, aren't you?

Knock, knock.
Who's there?
Banana.
Banana who?
Banana split so ice-creamed.

Knock, knock.
Who's there?
Danielle.
Danielle who?
Danielle at me, it's not my fault.

Knock, knock.
Who's there?
Jackson.
Jackson who?
Jackson the telephone, you'd better
come and speak to him.

Knock, knock.
Who's there?
Deena.
Deena who?
Deena hear you the first time.

Knock, knock.
Who's there?
Iran.
Iran who?
Iran away when you answered before.

Knock, knock.
Who's there?
Ivan.
Ivan who?
Ivan U. Hat, do
you like it?

Knock, knock.
Who's there?
Betty.
Betty who?
Betty doesn't know who I am.

Knock, knock.
Who's there?
Meg.
Meg who?
Meg your bed before
you get any breakfast.

Knock, knock.
Who's there?
You.
You who?
You who! Is there anybody in?

Knock, knock.
Who's there?
Quacker.
Quacker who?
Quacker 'nother bad joke and I'm off!

Knock, knock.
Who's there?
Agatha.
Agatha who?
Agatha headache. Got an aspirin?

Knock, knock.
Who's there?
Donna Mae.
Donna Mae who?
Donna Mae Kew an offer you can't refuse.

Knock, knock.
Who's there?
Bolivia.
Bolivia who?
Bolivia me, I know what I'm talking
about.

Knock, knock.
Who's there?
Jimmy.
Jimmy who?
Jimmy a little kiss on the cheek.

Knock, knock.
Who's there?
Nurse.
Nurse who?
Nurse sense in
talking to you.

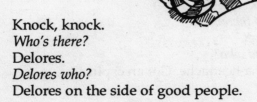

Knock, knock.
Who's there?
Delores.
Delores who?
Delores on the side of good people.

Knock, knock.
Who's there?
Nana.
Nana who?
Nana your business.

Knock, knock.
Who's there?
Frank.
Frank who?
Frank Lee, I don't care.

Knock, knock.
Who's there?
Quiet Tina.
Quiet Tina who?
Quiet Tina court
room, please!

Knock, knock.
Who's there?
Anne.
Anne who?
Anne apple just fell on my head.

Knock, knock.
Who's there?
Cereal.
Cereal who?
Cereal pleasure to meet you.

Knock, knock.
Who's there?
Honeydew.
Honeydew who?
Honeydew you want come out tonight?

Knock, knock.
Who's there?
Stan.
Stan who?
Stan back, I'm going to sneeze.

Knock, knock.
Who's there?
Stanton.
Stanton who?
Stanton here in the cold is no fun.

Knock, knock.
Who's there?
Poker.
Poker who?
Poker and see
if she's awake.

Knock, knock.
Who's there?
Alex.
Alex who?
Alex the questions around here!

Knock, knock.
Who's there?
Ada.
Ada who?
First Ada Kit.

Knock, knock.
Who's there?
Justin.
Justin who?
Justin Quire who is at the door.

Knock, knock.
Who's there?
Abbot.
Abbot who?
Abbot time you opened this door!

Knock, knock.
Who's there?
Isabelle.
Isabelle who?
Isabelle out of order? I had to knock
hard.

Knock, knock.
Who's there?
Emma.
Emma who?
Emma glad you asked me that.

Knock, knock.
Who's there?
Elsie.
Elsie who?
Elsie you around.

Knock, knock.
Who's there?
Gopher.
Gopher who?
Gopher your gun, Sheriff.

Knock, knock.
Who's there?
Howell.
Howell who?
Howell you have your toast, with
marmalade or jam?

Knock, knock.
Who's there?
Wanda.
Wanda who?
Wanda around
while I climb in
through the window.

Knock, knock.
Who's there?
Dishes.
Dishes who?
Dishes the police,
open up!

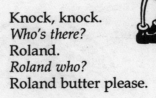

Knock, knock.
Who's there?
Roland.
Roland who?
Roland butter please.

Knock, knock.
Who's there?
Mabel.
Mabel who?
Mabel doesn't ring either.

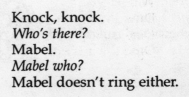

Knock, knock.
Who's there?
Ida.
Ida who?
Ida terrible time
getting here.

Knock, knock.
Who's there?
Irma.
Irma who?
Irma big girl now.

Knock, knock.
Who's there?
Iris.
Iris who?
Iris Tew in the name of the law.

Knock, knock.
Who's there?
N.E.
N.E. who?
N.E. body you like, as long as you let me
in.

Knock, knock.
Who's there?
Dino.
Dino who?
Dino the answer?

Knock, knock.
Who's there?
Lock.
Lock who?
Lock who it is, after
all this time!

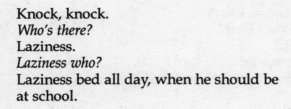

Knock, knock.
Who's there?
Oily.
Oily who?
The oily bird catches the worm.

Knock, knock.
Who's there?
Laziness.
Laziness who?
Laziness bed all day, when he should be
at school.

Knock, knock.
Who's there?
Pudding
Pudding who?
Pudding on your shoes
before your trousers is
a bad idea.

Knock, knock.
Who's there?
Eileen.
Eileen who?
Eileen Dover backwards.

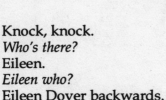

Knock, knock.
Who's there?
Jupiter.
Jupiter who?
Jupiter fly in my soup?

Knock, knock.
Who's there?
Tuna.
Tuna who?
Tuna violin and it will sound better.

Knock, knock.
Who's there?
Eileen.
Eileen who?
Eileen Don your bell and broke it.

Knock, knock.
Who's there?
Martin.
Martin who?
Martin of peas
won't open

Knock, knock.
Who's there?
Hijack.
Hijack who?
Hijack, how's Jill?

Knock, knock.
Who's there?
Lettuce.
Lettuce who?
Lettuce tell you a few good knock-knock
jokes.

Knock, knock.
Who's there?
Esther.
Esther who?
Esther anything I can do for you?

Knock, knock.
Who's there?
Noise.
Noise who?
Noise to see yer.

Knock, knock.
Who's there?
Denial.
Denial who?
Denial's a river in Egypt.

Knock, knock.
Who's there?
Luke.
Luke who?
Luke through the keyhole and see.

Knock, knock.
Who's there?
Kipper.
Kipper who?
Kipper your hands
to yourself.

Knock, knock.
Who's there?
Justice.
Justice who?
Justice I thought – no one at home.

Knock, knock.
Who's there?
Phyllis.
Phyllis who?
Phyllis in on the news.

Knock, knock.
Who's there?
Bruce.
Bruce who?
I Bruce very easily, don't hit me!

Knock, knock.
Who's there?
Adeline.
Adeline who?
Adeline extra to this letter.

Knock, knock.
Who's there?
Hosanna.
Hosanna who?
Hosanna Claus gets
down the chimney
I'll never know.

Knock, knock.
Who's there?
Ossia.
Ossia who?
Ossia on Monday night, OK?

Knock, knock.
Who's there?
Guthrie.
Guthrie who?
Guthrie blind mice.

Knock, knock.
Who's there?
Raleigh.
Raleigh who?
Raleigh round the flag, boys.

Knock, knock.
Who's there?
Adlai.
Adlai who?
Adlai a bet on that.

Knock, knock.
Who's there?
Punch.
Punch who?
Not me, please!

Knock, knock.
Who's there?
Canine.
Canien who?
Canine, L-10, M-11, N-12, O-12, O-13, P-14.....

Knock, knock.
Who's there?
Carrot.
Carrot who?
Knock, knock.
Who's there?
Carrot.
Carrot who?
Knock, knock.
Who's there?
Orange.
Orange who?
Orange you glad I didn't say carrot!

Knock, knock.
Who's there?
General Lee.
General Lee who?
General Lee I don't mind school dinners.

Knock, knock.
Who's there?
Boo.
Boo who?
Just boo! I'm a ghost!

Knock, knock.
Who's there?
Lionel.
Lionel who?
Lionel get you nowhere, better tell the truth.

Knock, knock.
Who's there?
Kent.
Kent who?
Kent you guess who it is?

Knock, knock.
Who's there?
Juno.
Juno who?
I dunno, Juno?

Knock, knock.
Who's there?
Thistle.
Thistle who?
Thistle be the last time
I knock on this door.

Knock, knock.
Who's there?
Allocate.
Allocate who?
Allocate, how are you dear?

Knock, knock.
Who's there?
Wooden shoe.
Wooden shoe who?
Wooden shoe like to know!

Knock, knock.
Who's there?
Heywood, Hugh and Harry.
Heywood, Hugh and Harry who?
Heywood Hugh Harry up and open this
door.

Knock, knock.
Who's there?
Huron.
Huron who?
Huron time for once.

Knock, knock.
Who's there?
Athena.
Athean who?
Athena flying thauther.

Knock, knock.
Who's there?
Moira.
Moira who?
Moira see you, Moira like you.

Knock, knock.
Who's there?
Aida.
Aida who?
Aida huge breakfast
before going to school.

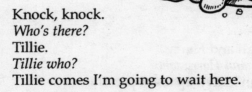

Knock, knock.
Who's there?
Tillie.
Tillie who?
Tillie comes I'm going to wait here.

Knock, knock.
Who's there?
Homer.
Homer who?
Homer gain!

Knock, knock.
Who's there?
Hollis.
Hollis who?
Hollis forgiven, come home.

Knock, knock.
Who's there?
Thumping
Thumping who?
Thumping green and slimy
is climbing up your neck.

Knock, knock.
Who's there?
Thayer.
Thayer who?
Thayer thorry.

Knock, knock.
Who's there?
Andy.
Andy who?
Andy little gadgets, door
knockers.

Knock, knock.
Who's there?
Minature.
Minature who?
Minature open your mouth you put your
foot in it.

Knock, knock.
Who's there?
Nadia
Nadia who?
Nadia head if you understand what I'm saying.

Knock, knock.
Who's there?
Ivan.
Ivan who?
Ivan my money back.

Knock, knock.
Who's there?
Sir.
Sir who?
Sir View right!

Knock, knock.
Who's there?
Fangs.
Fangs who?
Fangs very much.

Knock, knock.
Who's there?
Census.
Census who?
Census Saturday we don't have to go to school.

Knock, knock.
Who's there?
Wendy.
Wendy who?
Wendy go? I never saw him.

Knock, knock.
Who's there?
Datsun.
Datsun who?
Datsun old joke.

Knock, knock.
Who's there?
Amos.
Amos who?
Amos Quito bit me on
the nose.

Knock, knock.
Who's there?
Enoch.
Enoch who?
Enoch and Enoch, but nobody opens the
door.

Knock, knock.
Who's there?
Dr.
Dr. who?
That's right!

Knock, knock.
Who's there?
Don Juan.
Don Juan who?
Don Juan to go out today?

Knock, knock.
Who's there?
Waddle.
Waddle who?
Waddle you give me to go away?

Knock, knock.
Who's there?
Yacht.
Yacht who?
Yachts up, Doc?

Knock, knock.
Who's there?
Watson.
Watson who?
Watson your head?

Knock, knock.
Who's there?
Wannetta.
Wannetta who?
Wannetta time, please!

Knock, knock.
Who's there?
Carlotta.
Carlotta who?
Carlotta trouble when it
breaks down.

Knock, knock.
Who's there?
Hugh.
Hugh who?
Hugh is going to let me in then?

Knock, knock.
Who's there?
Olive.
Olive who?
Olive you too, Honeybunch!

Knock, knock.
Who's there?
Carmen.
Carmen who?
Carmen get it!

Knock, knock.
Who's there?
Warner.
Warner who?
Warner you coming out to play?

Knock, knock.
Who's there?
Joan.
Joan who?
Joan call us, we'll call you.

Knock, knock.
Who's there?
Sadie.
Sadie who?
Sadie ten times table twice.

Knock, knock.
Who's there?
Ivan.
Ivan who?
Ivan idea you don't want to see me.

Knock, knock.
Who's there?
Clarkson.
Clarkson who?
Clarkson watches tell the time.

Knock, knock.
Who's there?
Sophie.
Sophie who?
Sophie come to the end of the lesson.

Knock, knock.
Who's there?
Darwin.
Darwin who?
I'll be Darwin you open the door.

Knock, knock.
Who's there?
Paul.
Paul who?
Paul hard, the door's stuck again.

Knock, knock.
Who's there?
Scold.
Scold who?
Scold outside.

Knock, knock.
Who's there?
Tennis.
Tennis who?
Tennis five plus
five.

Knock, knock.
Who's there?
Scott.
Scott who?
Scott nothing to do with you.

Knock, knock.
Who's there?
Nuisance.
Nuisance who?
What's Nuisance yesterday?

Knock, knock.
Who's there?
Hammond.
Hammond who?
Hammond cheese
on toast, please.

Knock, knock.
Who's there?
I'm sorry, but my mother doesn't allow
me to talk to strangers.

Knock, knock.
Who's there?
Emile.
Emile who?
Emile fit for a king.

Knock, knock.
Who's there?
One-eye.
One-eye who?
You're the One-eye care for.

Knock, knock.
Who's there?
Anna.
Anna who?
Anna Nother thing, how many times do I
have to knock on this door before you
open up?

Knock, knock.
Who's there?
Jess.
Jess who?
Jess me!

Knock, knock.
Who's there?
Howard.
Howard who?
Howard I know?

Knock, knock.
Who's there?
William.
William who?
William Enyd my bike
while I go to the shops?

Knock, knock.
Who's there?
Thumb.
Thumb who?
Thumb like it hot, thumb like it cold....

Knock, knock.
Who's there?
Norman.
Norman who?
Norman invasion was 1066.

Knock, knock.
Who's there?
Justin.
Justin who?
Justin time for dinner.

Knock, knock.
Who's there?
Chester.
Chester who?
Chester Minute! Don't
you recognise me?

Knock, knock.
Who's there?
Sultan.
Sultan who?
Sultan Pepper.

Knock, knock.
Who's there?
Dimension.
Dimension who?
Dimension it!

Knock, knock.
Who's there?
Toby.
Toby who?
Toby or not to be.

Knock, knock.
Who's there?
Thaddeus.
Thaddeus who?
Thaddeus the question.

Knock, knock.
Who's there?
Mr.
Mr who?
Mr last bus home again.

Knock, knock.
Who's there?
Nantucket.
Nantucket who?
Nantucket, but she'll have to give it back.

Knock, knock.
Who's there?
Fozzie.
Fozzie who?
Fozzie hundredth time, my name is Nigel!

Knock, knock.
Who's there?
Havelock.
Havelock who?
Havelock put on your door.

Knock, knock.
Who's there?
Donna.
Donna who?
Donna sit under the apple tree with
anyone else but me.

Knock, knock.
Who's there?
Meredith.
Meredith who?
Meredith kind of joke and I'm leaving.

Knock, knock.
Who's there?
Orange juice.
Orange juice who?
Orange juice going to talk to me?

Knock, knock.
Who's there?
Dozen.
Dozen who?
Dozen anybody want to play with me?

Knock, knock.
Who's there?
Oslo.
Oslo who?
Oslo down. What's the hurry?

Knock, knock.
Who's there?
Nick.
Nick who?
Nick R. Elastic.

Knock, knock.
Who's there?
Colleen.
Colleen who?
Colleen all cars!

Knock, knock.
Who's there?
Avon.
Avon who?
Avon to get in.

Knock, knock.
Who's there?
Cheese.
Cheese who?
Cheese a cute little girl.

Knock, knock.
Who's there?
Jupiter.
Jupiter who?
Jupiter hurry, or you'll miss the bus.

Knock, knock.
Who's there?
Stepfather who?
Stepfather who?
One stepfather and I'll be in.

Knock, knock.
Who's there?
Cash.
Cash who?
I didn't realise you were
some kind of nut.

Knock, knock.
Who's there?
Sam.
Sam who?
Sam person who knocked on the door last
time.

Knock, knock.
Who's there?
Bison.
Bison who?
Pudding Bison.

Knock, knock.
Who's there?
Trixie.
Trixie who?
Trixie couldn't do because
he was a bad magician.

Knock, knock.
Who's there?
Rosa.
Rosa who?
Rosa carrots grow in our garden.

Knock, knock.
Who's there?
Ooze.
Ooze who?
Ooze in charge around here?

Knock, knock.
Who's there?
Gopher.
Gopher who?
Gopher a long walk
off a short pier.

Knock, knock.
Who's there?
Viola.
Viola who?
Viola sudden you don't know me?

Knock, knock.
Who's there?
Savannah.
Savannah who?
Savannah you going to open the door?

Knock, knock.
Who's there?
Eliza.
Eliza who?
Eliza wake at night thinking about this
door.

Knock, knock.
Who's there?
Tennessee.
Tennessee who?
Tennessee you tonight?

Knock, knock.
Who's there?
Willy.
Willy who?
Willy make it? I bet he won't!

Knock, knock.
Who's there?
Warren.
Warren who?
Warren my birthday suit.

Knock, knock.
Who's there?
Genoa.
Genoa who?
Genoa new knock-knock joke?

Knock, knock.
Who's there?
Evadne.
Evadne who?
Evadne problems with
your teeth?

Knock, knock.
Who's there?
Sari.
Sari who?
Sari I was sarong.

Knock, knock.
Who's there?
Juanita.
Juanita who?
Juanita 'nother hot dog?

Knock, knock.
Who's there?
Sacha.
Sacha who?
Sacha lot of questions.

Knock, knock.
Who's there?
Emma.
Emma who?
Emma pig when it comes to ice-cream.

Knock, knock.
Who's there?
Beth.
Beth who?
Beth wisheth, thweetie!

Knock, knock.
Who's there?
Xavier.
Xavier who?
Xavier breath, I'm not leaving.

Knock, knock.
Who's there?
Felix.
Felix who?
Felix-ited all over.

Knock, knock.
Who's there?
Liza.
Liza who?
Liza wrong to tell.

Knock, knock.
Who's there?
Juicy.
Juicy who?
Juicy that rude sign on the door?

Knock, knock.
Who's there?
Willis.
Willis who?
Willis rain never end?

Knock, knock.
Who's there?
Earl.
Earl who?
Earl be glad to get
to bed, I'm tired.

Knock, knock.
Who's there?
Wayne.
Wayne who?
Wayne is coming through the woof.

Knock, knock.
Who's there?
Kermit.
Kermit who?
Kermit a crime and
you'll get locked up.

Knock, knock.
Who's there?
Wilma.
Wilma who?
Wilma dreams come true?

Knock, knock.
Who's there?
Lois.
Lois who?
Lois the opposite of high.

Knock, knock.
Who's there?
UCI.
UCI who?
UCI had to ring because
you didn't answer when
I knocked.

Knock, knock.
Who's there?
Morris.
Morris who?
Morris in the pot, help yourself.

Knock, knock.
Who's there?
Thermos.
Thermos who?
Thermos be a better way
to earn a living.

Knock, knock.
Who's there?
Snow.
Snow who?
Snow use, I've lost the little card with my name on it.

Knock, knock.
Who's there?
Ferdie.
Ferdie who?
Ferdie last time, open the door!

Knock, knock.
Who's there?
Eddie.
Eddie who?
Eddie Body home?

Knock, knock.
Who's there?
Boo.
Boo who?
Don't start crying.

Knock, knock.
Who's there?
Gwen.
Gwen who?
Gwen will I see you again?

Knock, knock.
Who's there?
Zone.
Zone who?
Zone shadow scares him.

Knock, knock.
Who's there?
Value.
Value who?
Value be my Valentine?

Knock, knock.
Who's there?
Cello.
Cello who?
Cello dere!

Knock, knock.
Who's there?
Alma.
Alma who?
Alma not going to tell you!

Knock, knock.
Who's there?
· Hugh.
Hugh who?
Hugh dunnit?

Knock, knock.
Who's there?
Althea.
Althea who?
Althea later this afternoon.

Knock, knock.
Who's there?
Alaska.
Alaska who?
Alaska my mummy.

Knock, knock.
Who's there?
Weavish.
Weavish who?
Weavish you a merry Christmas and a
happy New Year.

Knock, knock.
Who's there?
Warner.
Warner who?
Warner lift? My car's outside.

Knock, knock.
Who's there?
Adam.
Adam who?
Adam up and tell me the total.

Knock, knock.
Who's there?
Sincerely.
Sincerely who?
Sincerely this morning I've been waiting
for you to open this door.

Knock, knock.
Who's there?
Pencil.
Pencil who?
Your pencil fall down if
the elastic goes.

Knock, knock.
Who's there?
Custer.
Custer who?
Custer a penny to find out.

Knock, knock.
Who's there?
Nora.
Nora who?
Nora Bone.

Knock, knock.
Who's there?
Romeo.
Romeo who?
Romeo Ver to the other side of the lake.

Knock, knock.
Who's there?
Daisy.
Daisy who?
Daisy plays, nights he sleeps.

Knock, knock.
Who's there?
Zena.
Zena who?
Zena stealing my books.

Knock, knock.
Who's there?
Cyril.
Cyril who?
Cyril thing – no imitations here.

Knock, knock.
Who's there?
Tina.
Tina who?
Tina Pilchards.

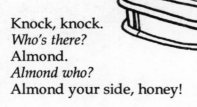

Knock, knock.
Who's there?
Almond.
Almond who?
Almond your side, honey!

Knock, knock.
Who's there?
Water
Water who?
Water be ashamed of yourself!

Knock, knock.
Who's there?
Jewel.
Jewel who?
Jewel remember me when you see my
face.

Knock, knock.
Who's there?
Tyrone.
Tyrone who?
Tyrone sheolaces,
you're old enough.

Knock, knock.
Who's there?
Miss.
Miss who?
Miss L. Toe is nice at Christmas.

Knock, knock.
Who's there?
Musket.
Musket who?
Musket in, it's urgent.

Knock, knock.
Who's there?
Fred.
Fred who?
Fred I can't come out tonight.

Knock, knock.
Who's there?
Oswald.
Oswald who?
Oswald my bubble gum.

Knock, knock.
Who's there?
Viscount.
Viscount who?
Viscount you behave yourself?

Knock, knock.
Who's there?
Wee Hiram.
Wee Hiram who?
Wee Hiram for a pound an
    hour.

Knock, knock.
Who's there?
Annetta.
Annetta who?
Annetta joke like that and you're off this
bus!

Knock, knock.
Who's there?
Owen.
Owen who?
Owen you open the door I've got
something for you.

Knock, knock.
Who's there?
Mitzi.
Mitzi who?
Mitzi door shut you'll never find out.

Knock, knock.
Who's there?
Mandy
Mandy who?
Mandy lifeboats,
we're sinking.

Knock, knock.
Who's there?
Lettuce.
Lettuce who?
Lettuce try again tomorrow.

Knock, knock.
Who's there?
Kenneth.
Kenneth who?
Kenneth little kid play with you?

Knock, knock.
Who's there?
Tuna.
Tuna who?
Tuna your radio down,
I'm trying to get some sleep.

Knock, knock.
Who's there?
Alda.
Alda who?
Alda time you knew who it was.

Knock, knock.
Who's there?
Marcella.
Marcella who?
Marcella's full of water.

Knock, knock.
Who's there?
Lionel.
Lionel who?
Lionel roar if you
don't feed him.

Knock, knock.
Who's there?
Eskimo.
Eskimo who?
Eskimo questions, I'll tell
you no lies.

Knock, knock.
Who's there?
Cargo.
Cargo who?
Cargo better if you fill it
with petrol first.

Knock, knock.
Who's there?
Howie.
Howie who?
Howie Dewin then?

Knock, knock.
Who's there?
Alfred.
Alfred who?
Alfred the needle
if you sew.

Knock, knock.
Who's there?
Ketchup.
Ketchup who?
Ketchup with me and I'll tell you.

Knock, knock.
Who's there?
Ahab.
Ahab who?
Ahab to go to the bathroom.

Knock, knock.
Who's there?
Toyota.
Toyota who?
Toyota be a law against knock-knock
jokes.

Knock, knock.
Who's there?
Ammonia.
Ammonia who?
Ammonia gonna tell you once.

Knock, knock.
Who's there?
Ralph.
Ralph who?
Ralph! Ralph! Ralph!
I'm your puppy dog.

Knock, knock.
Who's there?
Diploma.
Diploma who?
Diploma to fix the leak.

Knock, knock.
Who's there?
Bless.
Bless who?
I didn't sneeze.

Knock, knock.
Who's there?
Gilda.
Gilda who?
Gilda fly that sat on the
end of my nose.

Knock, knock.
Who's there?
Alice.
Alice who?
Alice forgiven, please come home.

Knock, knock.
Who's there?
Formosa.
Formosa who?
Formosa the summer I was away on
holiday.

Knock, knock.
Who's there?
Harris.
Harris who?
Harris nice to have on the top of your
head.

Knock, knock.
Who's there?
Spook.
Spook who?
Spook only when are spoken to.

Knock, knock.
Who's there?
Piglet.
Piglet who?
Piglet me in the last time I came.

Knock, knock.
Who's there?
Dana.
Dana who?
Dana talk with your mouth full.

Knock, knock.
Who's there?
Eyes.
Eyes who?
Eyes got loads more knock-knock jokes
for you.

Knock, knock.
Who's there?
Evadne.
Evadne who?
Evadne snails for tea?
They're horrible!

Knock, knock.
Who's there?
Virtue.
Virtue who?
Virtue get these big brown eyes?

Knock, knock.
Who's there?
Yacht.
Yacht who?
Yacht a know me by now.

Knock, knock.
Who's there?
Wicked.
Wicked who?
Wicked go for long walks together.

Knock, knock.
Who's there?
Omar.
Omar who?
Omar goodness! Wrong door!

Knock, knock.
Who's there?
Signor.
Signor who?
Signor light on, so I knocked.

Knock, knock.
Who's there?
Jethro.
Jethro who?
Jethro the boat and stop talking so much.

Knock, knock.
Who's there?
Warrior.
Warrior who?
Warrior been all my life?

Knock, knock.
Who's there?
Armageddon.
Armageddon who?
Armageddon out of here!

Knock, knock.
Who's there?
Hominy.
Hominy who?
Hominy people live in your house?

Knock, knock.
Who's there?
Moose.
Moose who?
Moose you be so nosey?

Knock, knock.
Who's there?
Patsy.
Patsy who?
Patsy dog on the head, he likes it.

Knock, knock.
Who's there?
Illegal.
Illegal who?
Illegals stay in the nest
until they feel better.

Knock, knock.
Who's there?
Barry.
Barry who?
Barry the treasure where no-one will find
it.

Knock, knock.
Who's there?
Lyndon.
Lyndon who?
Lyndon ear and I'll tell you.

Knock, knock.
Who's there?
Bean.
Bean who?
Bean working real hard today.

Knock, knock.
Who's there?
Dwayne.
Dwayne who?
Dwayne the bathtub, I'm dwowning.

Knock, knock.
Who's there?
I don't know.
I don't know who?
Neither do I, I keep telling you that.

Knock, knock.
Who's there?
Police.
Police who?
Police open up, I have
to go to the bathroom.

Knock, knock.
Who's there?
Wanda.
Wanda who?
Wanda off and you'll get lost.

Knock, knock.
Who's there?
Ammon.
Ammon who?
Ammon old hand at picking locks.

Knock, knock.
Who's there?
Lauren.
Lauren who?
Lauren order.

Knock, knock.
Who's there?
Theodore.
Theodore who?
Theodore wasn't open so I knock-
knocked.

Knock, knock.
Who's there?
Heaven.
Heaven who?
Heaven seen you for a long time.

Knock, knock.
Who's there?
Arkansas.
Arkansas who?
Arkansas it, too!

Knock, knock.
Who's there?
Tibet.
Tibet who?
Early Tibet, early to rise.

Tap, tap.
Who's there?
Hurd.
Hurd who?
Hurd my hand, so I couldn't
knock-knock.

Knock, knock.
Who's there?
Fido.
Fido who?
Fido I have to wait here?

Knock, knock.
Who's there?
Andrew.
Andrew who?
Andrew all her money out of the bank.

Knock, knock.
Who's there?
Artichoke.
Artichoke who?
Artichoke when he swallowed his yo-yo.

Knock, knock.
Who's there?
Watson.
Watson who?
Watson the menu today?

Knock, knock.
Who's there?
Stu.
Stu who?
Stu late to ask questions.

Knock, knock.
Who's there?
Pecan.
Pecan who?
Pecan somebody your own size.

Knock, knock.
Who's there?
Diana.
Diana who?
Diana Mals are restless, open the cage.

Knock, knock.
Who's there?
Al.
Al who?
Al go home if you're not nice to me.

Knock, knock.
Who's there?
Tom Sawyer.
Tom Sawyer who?
Tom Sawyer underwear.

Knock, knock.
Who's there?
Zizi.
Zizi who?
Zizi when you know how.

Knock, knock.
Who's there?
Pasture.
Pasture who?
Pasture bedtime isn't it?

Knock, knock.
Who's there?
Arthur.
Arthur who?
Arthur any more biscuits left?

Knock, knock.
Who's there?
Dennis.
Dennis who?
Dennis says I need
a filling.

Knock, knock.
Who's there?
Consumption.
Consumption who?
Consumption be done about all these
knock-knock jokes?

Knock, knock.
Who's there?
Alice.
Alice who?
Alice N. Tew if you'll listen to me.

Knock, knock.
Who's there?
Ben.
Ben who?
Ben away a long time.

Knock, knock.
Who's there?
Uruguay.
Uruguay who?
Hugo Uruguay, and I'll go mine.

Knock, knock.
Who's there?
Mickey.
Mickey who?
Mickey dropped down the drain.

Knock, knock.
Who's there?
Colleen.
Colleen who?
Colleen up your room, it's filthy.

Knock, knock.
Who's there?
Harmon.
Harmon who?
Harmon your side.

Knock, knock.
Who's there?
Welcome.
Welcome who?
Welcome up and see me sometime.

Knock, knock.
Who's there?
Boxer.
Boxer who?
Boxer tricks.

Knock, knock.
Who's there?
Yukon.
Yukon who?
Yukon say that again.

Knock, knock.
Who's there?
Athena.
Athena who?
Athena reindeer
landing on your roof.

Knock, knock.
Who's there?
Cosy.
Cosy who?
Cosy who's knocking will you?

Knock, knock.
Who's there?
Harold.
Harold who?
Harold are you?

Knock, knock.
Who's there?
Jamaica.
Jamaica who?
Jamaica mistake?

Knock, knock.
Who's there?
Doughnut.
Doughnut who?
Doughnut open your presents until
Christmas Day.

    Knock, knock.
    Who's there?
    Olive.
    Olive who?
    Olive just around the corner.

Knock, knock.
Who's there?
Avenue.
Avenue who?
Avenue heard the good news?

    Knock, knock.
    Who's there?
    Juliet.
    Juliet who?
    Juliet the same amount but she's OK.

Knock, knock.
Who's there?
Tarzan.
Tarzan who?
Tarzan stripes forever.

Knock, knock.
Who's there?
Gus.
Gus who?
That's what you're supposed to do.

Knock, knock.
Who's there?
Olga.
Olga who?
Olga way when I'm good and ready.

Knock, knock.
Who's there?
Don.
Don who?
Don mess about, just open the door.

Knock, knock.
Who's there?
Santa.
Santa who?
Santa forward in our team was ill today.

Knock, knock.
Who's there?
Fiona.
Fiona who?
Fiona had something better to do, do you
think we'd hang around here?

Knock, knock.
Who's there?
Zippy.
Zippy who?
Mrs. Zippy.

Knock, knock.
Who's there?
Hugo.
Hugo who?
Hugo jump in the lake!

Knock, knock.
Who's there?
Osborne.
Osborne who?
Osborne today, it's my birthday.

Knock, knock.
Who's there?
Cattle.
Cattle who?
Cattle always purr when you stroke her.

Knock, knock.
Who's there?
Closure.
Closure who?
Closure mouth when you eat.

Knock, knock.
Who's there?
Zenia.
Zenia who?
Zenia on TV in that
commercial.

Knock, knock.
Who's there?
Sis.
Sis who?
Sis any way to treat a friend?

Knock, knock.
Who's there?
Cynthia.
Cynthia who?
Cynthia been gone I mith you very much.

Knock, knock.
Who's there?
Bingo.
Bingo who?
Bingo Ing to come and see you for ages.

Knock, knock.
Who's there?
Fred.
Fred who?
Fred I'll have to be going soon.

Knock, knock.
Who's there?
Titus.
Titus who?
Titus it can be.

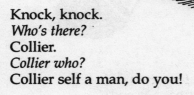

Knock, knock.
Who's there?
Collier.
Collier who?
Collier self a man, do you!

Knock, knock.
Who's there?
Four eggs.
Four eggs who?
Four eggs ample.

Knock, knock.
Who's there?
Gladys.
Gladys who?
Gladys E. Yew.

Knock, knock.
Who's there?
Razor.
Razor who?
Razor hands – this is a stick-up!

Knock, knock.
Who's there?
Dinah.
Dinah who?
Dinah is served.

Knock, knock.
Who's there?
Amy.
Amy who?
Amy fraid I've forgotten.

Knock, knock.
Who's there?
Ice-cream.
Ice-cream who?
Ice-cream and scream and
scream until I'm sick

Knock, knock.
Who's there?
Ella Mann.
Ella Mann who?
Ella Mann-Tree, my dear Watson.

Knock, knock.
Who's there?
Dinahmite.
Dinahmite who?
Dinahmite if you ask her nicely.

Knock, knock.
Who's there?
Tobias.
Tobias who?
Tobias a pig, that's why I went to market.

Knock, knock.
Who's there?
Sigrid.
Sigrid who?
Sigrid serivce – open up.

    Knock, knock.
    Who's there?
    Luke.
    Luke who?
    Luke before you leap.

Knock, knock.
Who's there?
Harvey.
Harvey who?
Harvey gonna play this game forever?

Knock, knock.
Who's there?
Kanga.
Kanga who?
No, kangaroo.

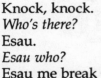

Knock, knock.
Who's there?
Esau.
Esau who?
Esau me break the window, so let me in
quick!

Knock, knock.
Who's there?
Wash.
Wash who?
Wash you there, Alice?

Knock, knock.
Who's there?
Freddie.
Freddie who?
Freddie or not, here I come!

Knock, knock.
Who's there?
Les.
Les who?
Les go out for a picnic.

Knock, knock.
Who's there?
Hans.
Hans who?
Hans up!

Knock, knock.
Who's there?
Seymour.
Seymour who?
Seymour if you look out of the window.

Knock, knock.
Who's there?
Blue.
Blue who?
Blue your nose.

Knock, knock.
Who's there?
Caesar.
Caesar who?
Caesar jolly good fellow.

Knock, knock.
Who's there?
Lief.
Lief who?
Lief me alone.

Knock, knock.
Who's there?
Andrew.
Andrew who?
Andrew a picture of Avril that hurt her
feelings.

Knock, knock.
Who's there?
Zeke.
Zeke who?
Zeke and ye shall find.

Knock, knock.
Who's there?
Chesterfield.
Chesterfield who?
Chesterfield full of cows, nothing else.

Knock, knock.
Who's there?
Alma.
Alma who?
Alma sweets have gone.

Knock, knock.
Who's there?
Yoga.
Yoga who?
Yoga what it takes.

Knock, knock.
Who's there?
Tank.
Tank who?
No, tank you!

Knock, knock.
Who's there?
Barbara.
Barbara who?
Barbara black sheep, have you any wool?

Knock, knock.
Who's there?
Bruce.
Bruce who?
I Bruce very easily.

Knock, knock.
Who's there?
Man.
Man who?
Man aged to get here then.

Knock, knock.
Who's there?
Heidi Clare.
Heidi Clare who?
Heidi Clare war on you.

Knock, knock.
Who's there?
Ooze.
Ooze who?
Ooze been sleeping in my bed?

Knock, knock.
Who's there?
Doughnut.
Doughnut who?
Doughnut let anyone else in but me.

Knock, knock.
Who's there?
Saul.
Saul who?
Saul over town we went to the movies together.

Knock, knock.
Who's there?
Rita.
Rita who?
Rita good book, you might learn
something.

Knock, knock.
Who's there?
Midas.
Midas who?
Midas well relax. I'm not
going anywhere.

Knock, knock.
Who's there?
Zookeeper.
Zookeeper who?
Zookeeper way from me!

Knock, knock.
Who's there?
Dorrie.
Dorrie who?
Dorrie I updet you.

Knock, knock.
Who's there?
Statue.
Statue who?
Statue? This is me.

Knock, knock.
Who's there?
Eddie.
Eddie who?
Eddie Body in there?

Knock, knock.
Who's there?
John.
John who?
John me in a cup of tea.

Knock, knock.
Who's there?
July.
July who?
July to me about stealing my pencil.

Knock, knock.
Who's there?
Weevil.
Weevil who?
Weevil only be staying a
minute.

Knock, knock.
Who's there?
Zoom
Zoom who?
Zoom did you expect?

Knock, knock.
Who's there?
Franz.
Franz who?
Franz, Romans, countrymen,
lend me your ears.

Knock, knock.
Who's there?
Betty.
Betty who?
Betty things to do than stand here, you
know.

Knock, knock.
Who's there?
Dick.
Dick who?
Dick potatoes out of the ground.

Knock, knock.
Who's there?
Sarah.
Sarah who?
Sarah 'nother way into this building?

Knock, knock.
Who's there?
Lady.
Lady who?
Lady law down.

Knock, knock.
Who's there?
Xavier.
Xavier who?
Xavier money for a rainy day.

Knock, knock.
Who's there?
Eiffel.
Eiffel who?
Eiffel out of the tower.

Knock, knock.
Who's there?
Aunt Lou.
Aunt Lou who?
Aunt Lou tired of knocking on this door?

Knock, knock.
Who's there?
Moses.
Moses who?
Moses will you come
and have tea with us?

Knock, knock.
Who's there?
Russian.
Russian who?
Russian about makes me tired.

Knock, knock.
Who's there?
Alpaca.
Alpaca who?
Alpaca picnic lunch.

Knock, knock.
Who's there?
Indonesia.
Indonesia who?
When I look at you I get weak Indonesia.

Knock, knock.
Who's there?
Amory.
Amory who?
Amory Christmas and a happy New Year
to all our readers.

Knock, knock.
Who's there?
Freighter.
Freighter who?
Freighter open the door?

Knock, knock.
Who's there?
Irish.
Irish who?
Irish you would come out and play with
me.

      Knock, knock.
      Who's there?
      Allied.
      Allied who?
      Allied, I'm sorry.

Knock, knock.
Who's there?
Moppet.
Moppet who?
Moppet up before it gets sticky.

Knock, knock.
Who's there?
Sibyl.
Sibyl who?
Sibyl Simon met a pieman going to the
fair.

Knock, knock.
Who's there?
Arizona.
Arizona who?
Arizona room for one of us.

Knock, knock.
Who's there?
Toothy.
Toothy who?
Toothy ith the day before
Wednethday.

Knock, knock.
Who's there?
Anatole.
Anatole who?
Anatole me you're a
pain in the neck.

Knock, knock.
Who's there?
Izzy.
Izzy who?
Izzy come, izzy go.

Knock, knock.
Who's there?
Noah.
Noah who?
Noah yes – which is it?

Knock, knock.
Who's there?
Orange juice.
Orange juice?
Orange juice sorry you asked?

Knock, knock.
Who's there?
Stan.
Stan who?
Stan back, I'm knocking the door down.

Knock, knock.
Who's there?
Webster.
Webster who?
Webster Spin, the spider.

Knock, knock.
Who's there?
Duck.
Duck who?
Just duck! They're throwing things at us.

Knock, knock.
Who's there?
Boiler.
Boiler who?
Boiler egg for four minutes.

Knock, knock.
Who's there?
Nettie.
Nettie who?
Nettie as a fruitcake.

Knock, knock.
Who's there?
Uriah.
Uriah who?
Keep Uriah on
the ball.

Knock, knock.
Who's there?
Cellar.
Cellar who?
Cellar? No, I think she can be repaired.

Knock, knock.
Who's there?
Jessica.
Jessica who?
Jessica than I thought. I'll get a doctor.

Knock, knock.
Who's there?
Orson.
Orson who?
Orson Cart.

Knock, knock.
Who's there?
Lion.
Lion who?
Lion down on the job.

Knock, knock.
Who's there?
Emmett.
Emmett who?
Emmett the back door, not the front.

Knock, knock.
Who's there?
Waldo.
Waldo who?
Waldo the washing-up in the morning.

Knock, knock.
Who's there?
Bridget.
Bridget who?
London Bridget falling down.

Knock, knock.
Who's there?
Roland.
Roland who?
Roland stone gathers no moss.

Knock, knock.
Who's there?
Ivan.
Ivan who?
It's not Ivan who, it's
Ivanhoe.

Knock, knock.
Who's there?
Gino.
Gino who?
Gino me? Then open the door!

Knock, knock.
Who's there?
Beats.
Beats who?
Beats me, I just forgot the joke.

Knock, knock.
Who's there?
Max.
Max who?
Max no difference, just open the door.

Knock, knock.
Who's there?
Howell.
Howell who?
Howell I get in if you don't open the door?

Knock, knock.
Who's there?
Congo.
Congo who?
We Congo on meeting like this.

Knock, knock.
Who's there?
Egypt.
Egypt who?
Egypt a bit off my best china plate.

Knock, knock.
Who's there?
Weirdo.
Weirdo who?
Weirdo you think you're going?

Knock, knock.
Who's there?
Anthea.
Anthea who?
Anthea get home by 8 o'clock, or else!

Knock, knock.
Who's there?
Harmony.
Harmony who?
Harmony knock-knock jokes do you
expect me to know?

Knock, knock.
Who's there?
Gorilla.
Gorilla who?
Gorilla me a hamburger.

Knock, knock.
Who's there?
Bertha.
Bertha who?
Bertha-day greetings.

Knock, knock.
Who's there?
Hiram.
Hiram who?
Hiram fine, how are you?

Knock, knock.
Who's there?
Major.
Major who?
Major answer the knock-knock joke!

Knock, knock.
Who's there?
Dummy.
Dummy who?
Dummy a favour and get lost.

Knock, knock.
Who's there?
Cynthia.
Cynthia who?
Cynthia been away so much has
happened.

Knock, knock.
Who's there?
Passion.
Passion who?
Just passion by and thought I'd pop in.

Knock, knock.
Who's there?
Watson.
Watson who?
Watson you mind? Tell me.

Knock, knock.
Who's there?
Dawn.
Dawn who?
Dawn do anything I wouldn't do.

Knock, knock.
Who's there?
Armenia.
Armenia who?
Armenia every word I say.

Knock, knock.
Who's there?
Ozzie.
Ozzie who?
Ozzie you later, OK?

Knock, knock.
Who's there?
Torch.
Torch who?
Torch you would never ask.

Knock, knock.
Who's there?
Jack.
Jack who?
Jack Potts.

Knock, knock.
Who's there?
Wayne.
Wayne who?
Wayne are you coming over to my house?

Knock, knock.
Who's there?
Olivia.
Olivia who?
Olivia me alone!

Knock, knock.
Who's there?
Gwendoline.
Gwendoline who?
Gwendoline out of the window and see
who's knocking.

Knock, knock.
Who's there?
Phineas.
Phineas who?
Phineas thing happened to me on the way
here.

Knock, knock.
Who's there?
Adore.
Adore who?
Adore stands between us, open up!

Knock, knock.
Who's there?
Seymour.
Seymour who?
Seymour if you had a pane of glass in
your door.

Knock, knock.
Who's there?
Sofa.
Sofa who?
Sofa we haven't made any mistakes.

Knock, knock.
Who's there?
Colin.
Colin who?
Colin the doctor, I'm not well.

Knock, knock.
Who's there?
Wheelbarrow.
Wheelbarrow who?
Wheelbarrow a car and go on a
trip.

Knock, knock.
Who's there?
Paul Lee.
Paul Lee who?
Feeling Paul Lee, so stayed in bed.

Knock, knock.
Who's there?
Izzie.
Izzie who?
Izzie at the door? You'd better answer it
then.

Knock, knock.
Who's there?
P.
P. who?
P. Nuts are an elephant's favourite treat.

Knock, knock.
Who's there?
Lass.
Lass who?
That's what cowboys use, isn't it?

Knock, knock.
Who's there?
Norman.
Norman who?
Norman has ever set foot here before.

Knock, knock.
Who's there?
Matthew.
Matthew who?
Matthew is pinching ma foot.

Knock, knock.
Who's there?
Ken.
Ken who?
Ken I. Cummin, it's freezing out here?

Knock, knock.
Who's there?
Custer.
Custer who?
Custer Diss nice with prunes.

Knock, knock.
Who's there?
Witch.
Witch who?
Witch way to London?

Knock, knock.
Who's there?
Tinker.
Tinker who?
Tinker bell is out of order.

Knock, knock.
Who's there?
Tilly.
Tilly who?
Tilly vision is my favourite invention.

Knock, knock.
Who's there?
Hannah.
Hannah who?
Hannah partridge in a pear tree.

Knock, knock.
Who's there?
Ireland.
Ireland who?
Ireland you a book if you promise to return it.

Knock, knock.
Who's there?
Alice.
Alice who?
I'm Alice standing here on your doorstep!

Knock, knock.
Who's there?
Deceit.
Deceit who?
Deceit of your trousers looks wet.

Knock, knock.
Who's there?
Don Juan.
Don Juan who?
Don Juan to stay here forever?

Knock, knock.
Who's there?
Safari.
Safari who?
Safari so good.

Knock, knock.
Who's there?
Alec.
Alec who?
Alec Tricity is shocking.

Knock, knock.
Who's there?
Carrie.
Carrie who?
Carrie me home, I'm tired.

Knock, knock.
Who's there?
Howard.
Howard who?
Howard the ground is when you slip on a
banana skin.

Knock, knock.
Who's there?
Stopwatch.
Stopwatch who?
Stopwatch you're doing this instant!

Knock, knock.
Who's there?
Lisa.
Lisa who?
Lisa you can do is let me in.

Knock, knock.
Who's there?
Jaws.
Jaws who?
Jaws truly.

Knock, knock.
Who's there?
Lucy.
Lucy who?
Lucy Lastic can be embarrassing.

Knock, knock.
Who's there?
Lena.
Lena who?
Lena little closer. I want to tell you a
secret.

Knock, knock.
Who's there?
Cameron.
Cameron who?
Cameron film are needed to take pictures.

Knock, knock.
Who's there?
Theresa.
Theresa who?
Theresa fly in my soup.

Knock, knock.
Who's there?
Yukon.
Yukon who?
Yukon go away and come back later.

Knock, knock.
Who's there?
Dunce.
Dunce who?
Dunce A. another word.

Knock, knock.
Who's there?
Arfer.
Arfer who?
Arfer Gott.

Knock, knock.
Who's there?
Fiddlestick.
Fiddlestick who?
Fiddlestick out of the
bottom of the bed if
you're too tall.

Knock, knock.
Who's there?
Sharon.
Sharon who?
Sharon share alike.

Knock, knock.
Who's there?
Auto.
Auto who?
Auto know, but I've forgotten.

Knock, knock.
Who's there?
Henrietta.
Henrietta who?
Henrietta hat
because he lost a bet.

Knock, knock.
Who's there?
Hanover.
Hanover who?
Hanover the money!

Knock, knock.
Who's there?
Asia.
Asia who?
Asia going to invite me in?

Knock, knock.
Who's there?
Russell.
Russell who?
Russell up something to eat.

Knock, knock.
Who's there?
Phoebe.
Phoebe who?
Phoebe too high for us to pay.

Knock, knock.
Who's there?
Goose.
Goose who?
Goose who's knocking at your door?

Knock, knock.
Who's there?
Gerald.
Gerald who?
Gerald friend again!

Knock, knock.
Who's there?
Lucinda.
Lucinda who?
Lucinda chain, I want to get in.

Knock, knock.
Who's there?
Fatso.
Fatso who?
Fatso matter with you?

Knock, knock.
Who's there?
Hope.
Hope who?
Hope Fully that present is for me.

Knock, knock.
Who's there?
Handsome.
Handsome who?
Handsome sweets through the door and
I'll tell you more.

Knock, knock.
Who's there?
Scold.
Scold who?
Scold enough for snow.

Knock, knock.
Who's there?
Elsie.
Elsie who?
Elsie you later.

Knock, knock.
Who's there?
Diesel.
Diesel who?
Diesel be your bags on the step, I
suppose?

124

Knock, knock.
Who's there?
Justin.
Justin who?
Justin Casey howls, give
him his bottle.

Knock, knock.
Who's there?
Fodder.
Fodder who?
Fodder and mother are taking me on
holiday.

Knock, knock.
Who's there?
Eustace.
Eustace who?
Come Eustace you are.

Knock, knock.
Who's there?
Dai.
Dai who?
Dai Larfin.

Knock, knock.
Who's there?
Hacienda.
Hacienda who?
Hacienda the book.

Write your own Knock Knocks...

Knock, Knock.
Who's there?
Doris.
Doris who?
Doris dropping off
its hinges with all
this knocking.

Other fun titles available from Madcap Books

All these books are available at your local bookshop or can be ordered direct from Littlehampton Book Services, 10-14 Eldon Way, Littlehampton, West Sussex, BN17 7HE. Tel: 01903 721596, fax: 01903 730828